Where Are You, Sun Bear?

Written by Eun-mi Choi
Illustrated by Seong-bin Noh
Edited by Joy Cowley

big & SMALL

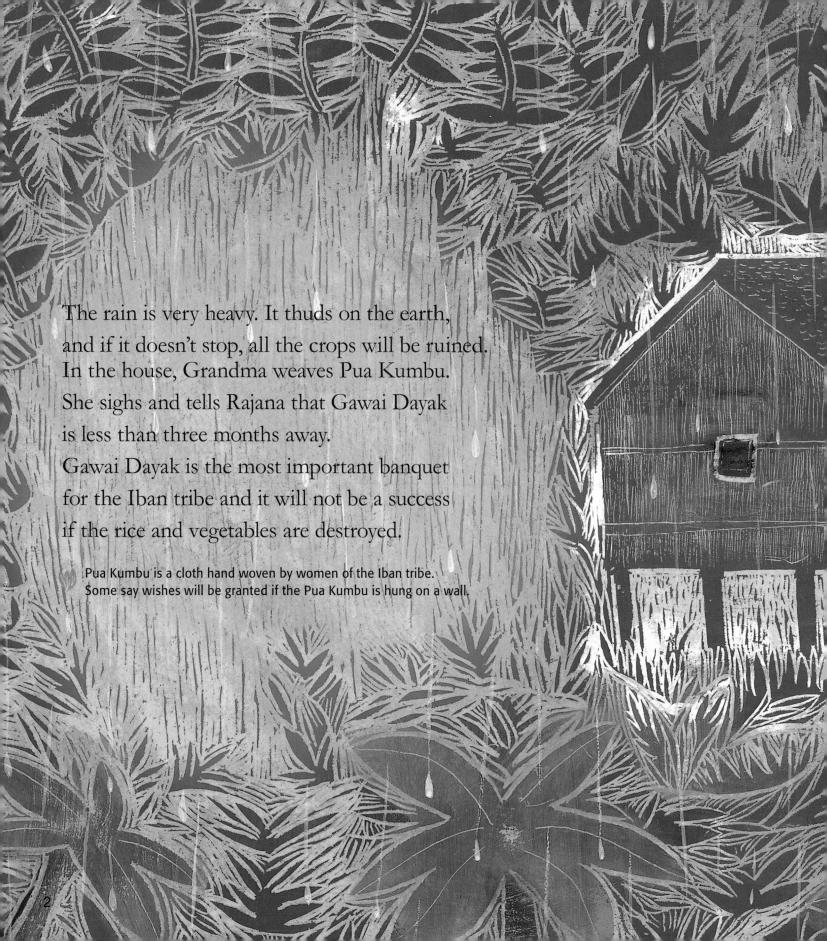

The rain is very heavy. It thuds on the earth,
and if it doesn't stop, all the crops will be ruined.
In the house, Grandma weaves Pua Kumbu.
She sighs and tells Rajana that Gawai Dayak
is less than three months away.
Gawai Dayak is the most important banquet
for the Iban tribe and it will not be a success
if the rice and vegetables are destroyed.

Pua Kumbu is a cloth hand woven by women of the Iban tribe.
Some say wishes will be granted if the Pua Kumbu is hung on a wall.

Rajana looks at the bear on the Pua Kumbu.
"Granny, there is a crescent shape
on the bear's chest. Why is it there?"

"That represents the sun, my dear.
That is why this bear is called a sun bear."

Rajana asks, "Will the rain stop
if the sun bear comes?"

"I'm not sure," says Granny.
"Perhaps the chief might know."

Rajana asks the chief,
"Where is the sun bear?"

"It is in the deep jungle,"
replies the chief.

"Is it a really big bear?"

"No, no," says the chief.
"It is the smallest bear in the world.
When the sun bear is fully grown,
it is only as big as you."

The jungle is a tropical forest with
large trees closely packed together.

7

That night, Grandma tells Rajana a story.
"Do you know what a Tua is?
It is a guardian that protects us.
The forest fairies send a Tua
to each one of us Iban people."

"What is your Tua, Grandma?"

"My Tua is the hornbill,"
replies Grandma.

"Then what about my Tua?"
asks Rajana.

"It will appear to you in a
dream," says Grandma.
"Let's sleep now."

The next day,
Rajana goes into the jungle
looking for the sun bear.
The jungle looks different.

10

First, she meets Grandma's hornbill.
"Hornbill, where will I find the sun bear?"

"Why do you want to know?"
asks the hornbill.

"It is said the sun bear brings out the sun.
If the sun shines, the crops will grow."

The hornbill says,
"Ask the Malayan tapir.
It knows where everyone is.
The tapir lives in the middle
of this deep jungle."

Rajana walks and walks and walks
but there is no sign of the Malayan tapir.
Weary, she sits on the ground.
There is a strange noise behind a tree.

"Are you the Malayan tapir?" she asks.

"Who are you?" asks the surprised tapir.

"I'm Rajana. I'm looking for the sun bear."

The Malayan tapir says, "It's a long time
since I last saw the sun bear.
But follow this little stream
and you will meet the long-nosed monkey.
It will know where the sun bear is."

15

Rajana follows
the little stream
until she comes to
the long-nosed monkey.
"What is a human child
doing in this place?"
says the long-nosed monkey.

"I need to see the sun bear.
The sun bear will bring back the sun."

The long-nosed monkey scratches itself.
"The sun bear is very angry
because trees have been cut down .
He is in a place far from here
and he has hidden the sun with him.
That is why it rains every day."

Rajana keeps on walking
but everywhere she looks
she sees trees that have been cut.
Rajana is exhausted.
She falls down on the earth.

Rajana hears footsteps and opens her eyes.
"Sun bear?" she says, reaching toward it.

The sun bear looks at her and says,
"People have destroyed the jungle.
I have to find a home full of trees."

Then the sun bear disappears.

Rajana calls, "Sun bear! Don't leave!"

"Rajana! Are you okay, my dear?"

Rajana opens her eyes.
Grandma is holding her
and her family is worried.

"Granny, I met the sun bear.
It said humans destroyed the forest.
If we keep cutting down trees,
we might never see the sun bear again."

Grandma hugs Rajana,
and doesn't say a word.

Grandma wakes Rajana early,
and points at the window.
The golden sun is shining.

Grandma's new Pua Kumbu
is hanging on the wall.
The sun bear on the Pua Kumbu
looks as though it is smiling.

"Thank you, sun bear," says Rajana.
"Thank you, my Tua."

24

About Malaysia
Malaysia, Where Nature Breathes

The Malaysian flag is blue, white, red and yellow. The blue square represents the unity of the nation. The yellow is the royal color of the Malay rulers. The crescent shape is a symbol of Islam and the star represents the federation of its states.

Asia's Amazon - the Malaysian Rainforest

More than half of Malaysia is covered in rainforest. The oxygen released here goes into the atmosphere and helps people to breathe. That is why the Malaysian rainforest is called "Asia's Amazon." However, as the Malaysian economy develops, the rainforest is being destroyed. If this continues, the oxygen needed to breathe will decrease and many animals will disappear.

Hand-woven Pua Kumbu

The Iban tribe is in the state of Sarawak on the island of Borneo. The women of the Iban tribe weave a special type of cloth called Pua Kumbu. This cloth is dyed with natural plant dyes, in beautiful pastel colors. It is said there are no identical Pua Kumbus because each has different patterns. It takes about six months to weave one cloth.

A Pua Kumbu on a loom

Bird with a Big Bill

The hornbill Rajana first encountered has black feathers, but some have white patterns. This bird is called a hornbill because it has a very large beak and also a large horn on the bridge of its nose. Its voice is very loud. It eats bugs, mice and fruit on trees.

A black hornbill with white feathers

A black and white Malayan tapir

Malayan Tapir

The body of a Malayan tapir is black and white. It has a short tail. The nose and upper lip are joined together and move freely. It is a herbivore, eating grass, leaves and fruit.

Sun Bear

The sun bear is also called the Malayan bear. It is smaller than other bears and has a ring-shaped pattern on its chest in either white or orange. It has a long white tongue and eats fruit, small animals and insects.

East West Malaysia

Malaysia is separated into two parts. Western Malaysia is north of Singapore on the west peninsula, and Eastern Malaysia is on the island of Borneo. 80 per cent of Malaysians live in Western Malaysia. In Eastern Malaysia there are many small tribes, like the Iban tribe. Famous Malaysian national parks are mostly in Eastern Malaysia.

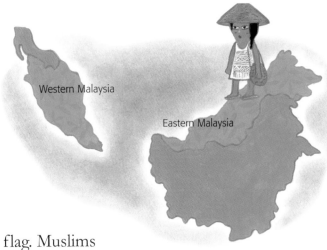

Western Malaysia

Eastern Malaysia

Country of the Yellow New Moon

Many Islamic countries have a new moon on their country's flag. Muslims believe that the new moon is the beginning of a new month.
Most Malaysians are Muslim but there are also people who are Buddhists, Christians, Hindus, and Sikhs in Malaysia. Malaysians live peacefully together.

Malaysian Twin Buildings

There are towers that look like twins in the capital city, Kuala Lumpur. They are called the "Petronas Tower Buildings." The towers are symbolic of the future of Malaysia. There is a bridge connecting the two towers to make sure the building does not shake.

The height of the Petronas Twin Towers is 452 meters

A statue of a Hindu god

Temple in Batu Cave

Batu Cave is a place visited by Hindu devotees. There is a temple inside a cave where Hindu mythology is drawn on the walls. A hole in the roof of the cave lets in the sunlight to illuminate the interior. Many wild monkeys and bats live in the cave.

Malaysia and Rubber

Malaysia produces a lot of natural rubber from the juice extracted from farmed rubber trees. Rubber is very important to the Malaysian economy. In the past, rubber was a major export. Now, goods like rubber gloves are made and sold to improve the economy.

South China Sea

Thailand

Langkawi

Penang Island

Kota Bharu

*Wat Chayamangkalaram
The Buddhist temple
famous for its Reclining
Buddha statue

*Petronas Twin Towers
Twin towers standing at 452 meters tall

*Malaysia

Kuantan

Kuala Lumpur

*Mangrove forests
A unique tropical ecosystem

Malacca

*Menara Telekom Tower
55 floor building which is shaped
like a sprouting bamboo shoot

Johor Bahru

Singapore

Kuc

Malaysia

Country name: Malaysia

Location: Southeast Asia

Area: 127,320 mi^2 (329,750 km^2)

Capital: Kuala Lumpur

Population: Approx. 29.27 million (2013)

Language: Malaysian

Main religion: Islam

Main exports: Electrical goods, natural gas, palm oil, natural rubber, wood

Kudat

*Sabah State Mosque
Islamic mosque and school

Tawau

*Deer Cave
One of the biggest natural caves in the world

Brunei

*Borneo Island

*Malaysia

Sibu

Indonesia

*Silat
Traditional martial arts

Original Korean text by Eun-mi Choi

Illustrations by Seong-bin Noh

Korean edition © Aram Publishing

This English edition published by big & SMALL in 2015

by arrangement with Aram Publishing

English text edited by Joy Cowley

English edition © big & SMALL 2015

Distributed in the United States and Canada by

Lerner Publishing Group, Inc.

241 First Avenue North

Minneapolis, MN 55401 U.S.A.

www.lernerbooks.com

ISBN: 978-1-925233-53-7

Printed in the United States of America

1 – CG – 5/31/15